DRAWING PROMPT JOURNAL FOR GIRLS

Little Red Hen produces books that combine beautiful design and positive psychology with a dash of humor to promote wellbeing and better living. Check out our full range by scanning the code below.

If you like this book, please give us a 5 star rating on Amazon.com - it means a lot!

Copyright © 2022 Little Red Hen
All rights reserved.
No portion of this book may be reproduced in any form without prior permission from the copyright owner of this book.

WELCOME

Drawing prompts are a fantastic way for kids (and adults!) to unleash their creativity. While free drawing is a wonderful activity for children, a blank page can be daunting. A drawing prompt narrows the possibilities and serves to trigger the imagination. The drawing prompts in this journal are open-ended enough to result in unique, creative artworks. In fact, the same prompt could, on different days, result in entirely different artworks depending on the child's mood, experiences or what they're currently interested in. It's amazing what just a pair of sunglasses on a white page can produce.

This book is intentionally simple to use. All that's required is some quiet time, drawing materials (crayons, pencils or pens) and this book opened to a particular page. For pre-reading children, an adult or older child will need to read them the written prompts but it's also fine to allow them to work from just the visual prompts and see where that goes. Possible ways to use this book include getting multiple copies and having friends or siblings work on the same prompt at the same time or how about laminating pages and using a felt tip pen that can be wiped off?

Drawing prompts develop drawing, thinking and storytelling skills but most importantly, they're fun!. So pick a page and let's get started!

FANCY A FREE DRAWING PROMPTS PRINTABLE FROM LITTLE RED HEN?

Just Scan, Subscribe & Download

Free Gift

**COMPLETE THE PICTURE.
DRAW SOME FLOWERS IN THIS VASE.**

Share this masterpiece with the world! Scan the code to post on our Facebook page.

COMPLETE THE PICTURE.
WHAT'S HAPPENING BENEATH THIS CRESCENT MOON?

Share this masterpiece with the world! Scan the code to post on our Facebook page.

COMPLETE THE PICTURE.
WHOSE LEGS ARE THESE? PERHAPS IT'S NOT WHAT WE'D EXPECT!

DRAW A STORY...
USE THIS MAGICAL CASTLE AS THE STARTING POINT FOR A STORY.

Share this masterpiece with the world! Scan the code to post on our Facebook page.

IT`S YOUR MASTERPIECE!
DRAW WHATEVER YOU LIKE WITHIN THE FANCY FRAME.

Share this masterpiece with the world! Scan the code to post on our Facebook page.

COMPLETE THE PICTURE.
WHO'S WEARING THESE HEART-SHAPED SUNGLASSES?

Share this masterpiece with the world! Scan the code to post on our Facebook page.

COMPLETE THE PICTURE.
DRAW SOMETHING ON THIS TREE BRANCH.

COMPLETE THE PICTURE.
WHO'S WEARING THIS PRETTY BALLERINA OUTFIT?

Share this masterpiece with the world! Scan the code to post on our Facebook page.

DRAW A STORY...
USE THIS MAGIC LANTERN AS THE STARTING POINT FOR A STORY.

Share this masterpiece with the world! Scan the code to post on our Facebook page.

IT'S YOUR MASTERPIECE!
DRAW WHATEVER YOU LIKE WITHIN THE FANCY FRAME.

Share this masterpiece with the world! Scan the code to post on our Facebook page.

COMPLETE THE PICTURE.
WHO'S WEARING THIS HAT? WHAT ARE THEY DOING?

Share this masterpiece with the world! Scan the code to post on our Facebook page.

COMPLETE THE PICTURE.
DRAW SOME PEOPLE ON THIS BALCONY.

Share this masterpiece with the world! Scan the code to post on our Facebook page.

COMPLETE THE PICTURE.

WHAT'S HAPPENING BENEATH THIS SHINING SUN?

Share this masterpiece with the world! Scan the code to post on our Facebook page.

DRAW A STORY...
USE THIS MAGIC WAND AS THE STARTING POINT.

Share this masterpiece with the world! Scan the code to post on our Facebook page.

IT'S YOUR MASTERPIECE!
DRAW WHATEVER YOU LIKE WITHIN THE FANCY FRAME.

Share this masterpiece with the world! Scan the code to post on our Facebook page.

**COMPLETE THE PICTURE.
WHO'S WEARING THIS TIARA?**

Share this masterpiece with the world! Scan the code to post on our Facebook page.

COMPLETE THE PICTURE.
DECORATE THESE BUTTERFLIES

Share this masterpiece with the world! Scan the code to post on our Facebook page.

COMPLETE THE PICTURE.
GIVE THIS BALLERINA A HEAD, BODY AND COSTUME.

Share this masterpiece with the world! Scan the code to post on our Facebook page.

DRAW A STORY...
USE THESE MAGICAL STARS AS A STARTING POINT.

Share this masterpiece with the world! Scan the code to post on our Facebook page.

IT'S YOUR MASTERPIECE!
DRAW WHATEVER YOU LIKE WITHIN THE FANCY FRAME.

Share this masterpiece with the world! Scan the code to post on our Facebook page.

COMPLETE THE PICTURE.
WHO'S WEARING THESE FLOWER-SHAPED SUNGLASSES?

Share this masterpiece with the world! Scan the code to post on our Facebook page.

COMPLETE THE PICTURE.
GIVE THIS UNICORN A BODY.

Share this masterpiece with the world! Scan the code to post on our Facebook page.

COMPLETE THE PICTURE.
WHAT'S AT THE END OF THIS RAINBOW?

Share this masterpiece with the world! Scan the code to post on our Facebook page.

DRAW A STORY...
USE THIS FAIRY AS A STARTING POINT.

Share this masterpiece with the world! Scan the code to post on our Facebook page.

IT'S YOUR MASTERPIECE!
DRAW WHATEVER YOU LIKE WITHIN THE FANCY FRAME.

Share this masterpiece with the world! Scan the code to post on our Facebook page.

COMPLETE THE PICTURE.
WHERE IS THIS BOW? ON A GIFT? ON SOMEONE'S HAIR? MAYBE ON A DRESS?

Share this masterpiece with the world! Scan the code to post on our Facebook page.

COMPLETE THE PICTURE.
WHO'S WEARING THESE GLASSES?

Share this masterpiece with the world! Scan the code to post on our Facebook page.

COMPLETE THE PICTURE.
WHAT'S HAPPENING AROUND THIS WISE OWL?

Share this masterpiece with the world! Scan the code to post on our Facebook page.

DRAW A STORY...
WHAT HAPPENED AFTER THE GENIE CAME OUT OF THE LAMP?

Share this masterpiece with the world! Scan the code to post on our Facebook page.

IT'S YOUR MASTERPIECE!
DRAW WHATEVER YOU LIKE WITHIN THE FANCY FRAME.

Share this masterpiece with the world! Scan the code to post on our Facebook page.

COMPLETE THE PICTURE.
ARE THESE FEATHERS PART OF A BIRD'S PLUMAGE? MAYBE THEY'RE DECORATION ON A HAT?

Share this masterpiece with the world! Scan the code to post on our Facebook page.

COMPLETE THE PICTURE.
WHAT'S HAPPENING UNDER THESE STAGE LIGHTS?

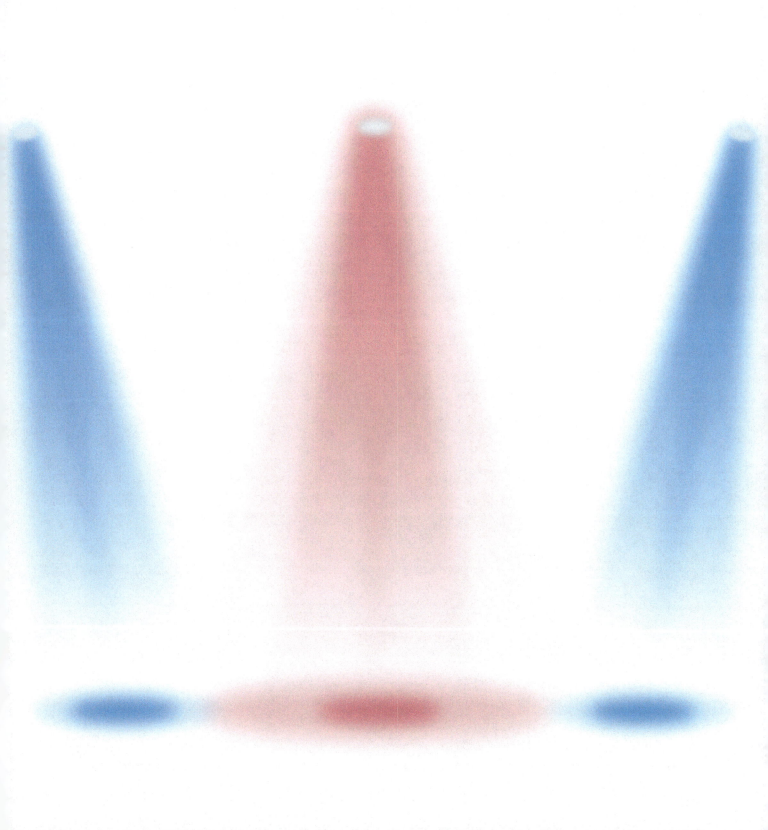

Share this masterpiece with the world! Scan the code to post on our Facebook page.

COMPLETE THE PICTURE.
GIVE THIS MERMAID A HEAD AND BODY. WHERE IS SHE?

Share this masterpiece with the world! Scan the code to post on our Facebook page.

DRAW A STORY...
USE THESE BUBBLES AS THE STARTING POINT.

Share this masterpiece with the world! Scan the code to post on our Facebook page.

IT'S YOUR MASTERPIECE!
DRAW WHATEVER YOU LIKE WITHIN THE FANCY FRAME.

Share this masterpiece with the world! Scan the code to post on our Facebook page.

COMPLETE THE PICTURE.
WHAT'S FALLING OUT OF THIS BAG?

Share this masterpiece with the world! Scan the code to post on our Facebook page.

COMPLETE THE PICTURE.
WHERE ARE THESE INSECTS FLYING? AMONGST FLOWERS & LONG GRASS, PERHAPS?

Share this masterpiece with the world! Scan the code to post on our Facebook page.

COMPLETE THE PICTURE.
IS SOMEONE THROWING A PARTY?

Share this masterpiece with the world! Scan the code to post on our Facebook page.

DRAW A STORY...
USE THIS MAGIC KEY AS THE STARTING POINT.

Share this masterpiece with the world! Scan the code to post on our Facebook page.

IT'S YOUR MASTERPIECE!
DRAW WHATEVER YOU LIKE WITHIN THE FANCY FRAME.

Share this masterpiece with the world! Scan the code to post on our Facebook page.

COMPLETE THE PICTURE.
WHO'S WEARING THIS BEAUTIFUL GOWN?

Share this masterpiece with the world! Scan the code to post on our Facebook page.

Share this masterpiece with the world! Scan the code to post on our Facebook page.

COMPLETE THE PICTURE.

WHO`S HOLDING THIS UMBRELLA? WHAT`S HAPPENING?

DRAW A STORY...
USE THIS TREASURE CHEST AS THE STARTING POINT.

Share this masterpiece with the world! Scan the code to post on our Facebook page.

IT'S YOUR MASTERPIECE!
DRAW WHATEVER YOU LIKE WITHIN THE FANCY FRAME.

Share this masterpiece with the world! Scan the code to post on our Facebook page.

COMPLETE THE PICTURE.
WHOSE EYES ARE THESE?

Share this masterpiece with the world! Scan the code to post on our Facebook page.

COMPLETE THE PICTURE.
WHO'S WEARING THESE PRETTY EARRINGS?

Share this masterpiece with the world! Scan the code to post on our Facebook page.

COMPLETE THE PICTURE.
WHO DO THESE WINGS BELONG TO?

COMPLETE THE PICTURE.
WHAT IS THIS GIRL DREAMING ABOUT?

Share this masterpiece with the world! Scan the code to post on our Facebook page.

IT'S YOUR MASTERPIECE!
DRAW WHATEVER YOU LIKE WITHIN THE FANCY FRAME.

Share this masterpiece with the world! Scan the code to post on our Facebook page.

Made in the USA
Las Vegas, NV
26 November 2023